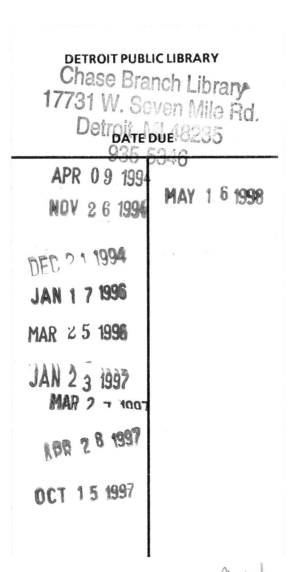

CH   NOV   1995

ON THE MAP

CANADA

Titles in This Series:

Canada	Russia
France	Spain
Italy	U.S.A.
Japan	West Indies

Editor: Frank Tarsitano
Design: M&M Partnership
Photographs: ZEFA except:
Allsport (27br); Canadian High Commission (18t); Canadian Tourist Office (20tr); Robert Estall (12l, 12b, 15tl, 27t); C. D. Flint (11tr, 20l, 29t); Hutchinson (17tl, 18 b); Spectrum (20br, 22t)
Map artwork: Raymond Turvey
Cover photo: *Canoeing on Moraine Lake, Banff National Park, Alberta*

Library of Congress Cataloging-in-Publication Data

Flint, David, 1946-
    Canada / written by David Flint.
       p. cm. — (On the map)
    Includes index.
    Summary: An illustrated introduction to the geography, people, education, daily life, sports, and famous landmarks of Canada.
    ISBN 0–8114–2939–3
    1. Canada — Juvenile literature. — [1.Canada.]
    I. Title.   II. Series.
    F1008.2.F57   1993
    917.1–dc20   92-43923
                                                   CIP   AC

Typeset by Multifacit Graphics, Keyport, NJ
Printed and bound in the United States
1 2 3 4 5 6 7 8 9 0 VH 98 97 96 95 94 93

CANADA

David Flint

RAINTREE STECK-VAUGHN
PUBLISHERS
The Steck-Vaughn Company

Austin, Texas

ARCTIC OCEAN

Arctic Circle

Miles
0 100 200 300 400 500
0 200 400 600 800
Kilometers

Hudson Bay

• Churchill

CANADIAN SHIELD

C A N A D A

Quebec City •

• Montreal
Ottawa •
Toronto •

Halifax •

ATLANTIC OCEAN

← St Lawrence Seaway

← Niagara Falls

Great Lakes

PRAIRIES

Edmonton •

Mt. Robson 12,972 ft. ▲

Takkakaw Falls •
Mt. Edith Cavell 11,034 ft. ▲
Lake Louise •
Mt. Victoria 11,365 ft. ▲
Calgary •

Rocky Mountains

Fraser River

Vancouver •

Dawson City •

▲ Mt. Logan 19,850 ft.

ALASKA

U S A

PACIFIC OCEAN

Contents

Wheat is grown on Canada's vast, flat Prairies.

Many Canadians live in large cities like Vancouver on the Pacific coast.

Icebreakers are used to get through the frozen water of the Arctic Ocean.

North Country

Canada is the world's second largest country. Only Russia is larger. Canada stretches from the Arctic Ocean in the north to the United States in the south. In the west, Canada meets the Pacific Ocean and in the east, it meets the Atlantic. The country is so wide from east to west that when it's noon on the east coast it is only seven in the morning on the west coast.

There are many different types of land in Canada. High, rugged mountains shoot skyward in the western part of the country. Cold, empty lands stretch across the north. Vast, fertile Prairies, thousands of lakes, and many beautiful rivers are all part of Canada.

Canada is located in the northern part of North America. It is a much colder country than most of the United States. The weather in the north is bitterly cold and freezing for nine months every year. Summers are short and cool. The south has cold winters, but they only last about three months. Summers here are hot, and most people live in the south. Many different types of crops are raised here.

Because the weather is better in southern Canada, most Canadians live there. Some of these Canadians live on farms and ranches, but most live in cities.

Mountains and Tundra

Long, high mountain ranges line Canada's Pacific coast. Canada's highest peak, Mt. Logan, is located in these Pacific mountain ranges. Mt. Logan is 19,850 feet high.

The Rocky Mountains are also in the western part of the country. The peaks of the Rockies are rugged and high. Some of them are covered in permanent ice and snow. Mt. Robson, at 12,972 feet, is only one of the many high peaks in the Canadian Rockies.

Not many people live in these mountains, but there are many rich natural resources here. Coal, silver, and other metals are mined in these mountains. There are also many forests here.

East of the Rockies is an area of wide plains. The southern part of these plains is called the Prairies. These lands are flat with few trees. The soil here is very good for farming and ranching. Forests grow in the northern part of the plains area.

To the north and east of the plains the land rises again to form a large area of lakes, swamps, and forests. This is called the Canadian Shield. In the far north is the tundra, a place where no trees grow.

A moose feeds on mosses and plants in a forest on the edge of the tundra in northern Canada. A fully grown moose can be over eight feet tall.

The Angel Glacier in Jasper National Park tumbles down the mountainside from the ice field above.

The vast, treeless tundra of northern Canada. At the end of the short summer, the mosses turn bright red and orange.

Lakes, Rivers, and Falls

The Great Lakes, in southeastern Canada are huge stretches of water. Canada shares four of the Great Lakes with the United States. These four lakes are Lake Huron, Lake Erie, Lake Ontario, and Lake Superior. These are used by thousands of ships.

At one time ships could not sail from the Great Lakes to the Atlantic Ocean. Then the St. Lawrence Seaway was built to connect the Great Lakes with the Atlantic Ocean. Now, oceangoing ships can sail far inland on the lakes to reach industrial towns like Toronto.

Many Canadian rivers flow north to Hudson Bay or the Arctic Ocean. Others, like the Fraser River, flow westward from the Rocky Mountains to the Pacific Ocean. Some of Canada's largest cities are on major rivers. The Fraser River flows to Canada's largest city on the Pacific coast, Vancouver. The St. Lawrence River in the east flows past Montreal and Quebec.

In the east, the Niagara River flows into Niagara Falls, one of the most famous falls in the world. The part of the falls that is in Canada is called the Horseshoe Falls, and the part that is in the United States is called the American Falls. Every year thousands of people from all over the world visit Niagara Falls.

A grizzly bear catches salmon at
a waterfall on the Fraser River
in British Columbia.

At Takkakaw Falls in Alberta the water
drops 1,142 feet. Takkakaw means "Wow!"
in the local Native American dialect.

Spirit Island on Maligne Lake in Alberta's Jasper National Park.
Maligne Lake is just one of Canada's many lakes.

The Mounties, with their famous red uniforms, are the national police force. They have a reputation of always catching criminals.

The town hall in Toronto, Ontario, is a fine example of modern architecture in Canada.

Nearly a third of the people speak French, so road signs are in both French and English.

Inuit children dress in thick furs to protect them in the freezing winter weather.

People and Provinces

The first Canadians were Native Americans and the Inuit. They lived in Canada for thousands of years before Europeans came. Today only about two percent of all Canadians are Native Americans and Inuits.

The first European settlers in Canada came from France. Few of these settlers were farmers. They were mostly hunters, soldiers, and trappers. Sailors from England explored some Canadian waterways. For example, Hudson Bay in northern Canada was named after Henry Hudson, who sailed for the English.

The French ruled Canada until 1763, when the English gained control of the country. Today about 45 percent of all Canadians have British ancestry and about 29 percent have French backgrounds. Today, English and French are Canada's two official languages. The remaining Canadians are Native Americans, the Inuit, or people whose ancestors came from other countries such as Italy or Germany.

Canada became an independent country in 1931. Today Canada is divided into ten provinces and two territories. Each province and territory has its own local government, schools, and police force. Canada's national government meets in Ottawa.

Great Riches

Canada is a country rich in natural resources. These resources include forests, minerals, and farmlands.

Canada's forests are harvested for lumber. Much of this lumber is turned into wood pulp. The wood pulp is then used to make paper. Canada is the world's leading supplier of a special paper called newsprint, the kind of paper used to make newspapers. Some of the wood is used as lumber for homes. The rest is used to make furniture and other wood products.

The best farmland is in the southern part of the country. These farms produce enough food to feed Canada's people with enough left over to sell to other countries. Wheat and cattle are raised on farms and ranches in Canada's Prairie Provinces. Canada is one of the world's leading producers of wheat. Many different fruits are raised in the western part of the country. The eastern farmlands are used to raise many different vegetables and dairy cattle.

Canada's mineral resources include asbestos, gold, iron, lead, nickel, potash, zinc, silver, and uranium. Oil and natural gas are two of Canada's most important mineral resources. Pipelines carry oil and natural gas from Alberta to the United States.

The Prairies of Alberta, Manitoba, and Saskatchewan produce most of Canada's wheat. Wheat is stored in huge grain elevators before being sent by rail to the towns.

About a third of Canada is covered by forest. Logs float down to sawmills, as here in British Columbia.

Asbestos is mined in big open pits like this one in Quebec. When the mining is finished the holes are filled in.

Oil from Alberta is refined in nearby Saskatchewan. Many things like gasoline and paint are made from oil.

Life in Canada

Canada is a large country with plenty of open space. Most Canadians live in or near cities, especially in the eastern part of the country. Canada has more than twenty cities with over 100,000 people. Montreal and Toronto each have more than two million people.

City life is fast and exciting. Stores open early in the morning and stay open until late at night. Some restaurants and stores never close. There are open-air cafés and very fine restaurants in those cities with a French background like Quebec.

Family life is important to Canadians. Families usually come together for their evening meal and share the events of the day. Children do their homework after they have eaten. Television is very popular, and Canadians receive many American shows.

Not all Canadians who live in rural areas are farmers. Many work in nearby cities and commute every day to and from their jobs.

Life in Canada's frozen northern lands can be very hard. Few people live in these areas, and life here has not changed much over the years. Inuit still hunt, fish, and trap wild animals in the Canadian north.

Corn eaten on the cob is popular
with Canadians of all ages.

Winters can be very cold, and sometimes
blizzards strike cities like Montreal.

Local artists display their work in
the Rue du Trésor (Treasure Street)
in Quebec.

Many Canadians spend their vacation
in the mountains, at places like
Moraine Lake in Alberta.

Public schools in Canada are free. This elementary school takes children from six to twelve years old.

Many children in Canada take school buses every day.

School Days

Each province and territory in Canada provides its own public schools, so all the schools are not alike. Children start school when they are six years old. When they are twelve, students go to junior high school. When they are fourteen they go on to high school.

Some provinces provide twelve years of education. Others provide eleven or thirteen years of schooling. Towns and cities pay for some of the education costs. The provinces and territories pay for the rest. Canada has private schools as well as public schools. The private schools charge for their services. There are also some separate church schools.

In the far north some children go to live-in schools. They stay there most of the year because they live such a long way from school.

Classes are usually taught in English, but in some areas classes are taught in French. The school year starts in September and ends in June. Students in Canada's schools study most of the same subjects that students in the United States study. Of course, Canadian students spend a great deal of time studying their own history.

Because distances in Canada are so vast, many people travel by air.

The Inuit find these motorbikes a big help in crossing the tundra.

Electric-powered trolleys are used in Vancouver to cut down on pollution from gasoline engines.

Railroads are important because they carry most of Canada's raw materials, such as lumber or iron ore.

Getting Around

Most people in Canada travel to work or go shopping in private cars. Southern Canada has many fine roads and highways for cars to travel on. Canada produces many of the cars used on the country's highways. Today, there is about one car for every two Canadians. Canadians use their cars for both business and pleasure.

Canada also has a good system of railroads. There are more than 50,000 miles of railroad track in Canada. Many modern railroads connect Canada's cities with its suburbs and rural areas. Every day thousands of Canadians commute back and forth to work on Canada's highways and railroads. Canadian trains also carry millions of tons of freight every year.

Since Canada is so large, airplanes are often used to get from one part of the country to another. Jet planes streak across Canadian skies connecting cities thousands of miles apart. Smaller planes are used for short flights.

The St. Lawrence Seaway joins the Great Lakes to the Atlantic Ocean. It is controlled jointly by Canada and the United States. The seaway stretches 2,485 miles inland, and ships carry wheat, coal, and iron.

The huge, flat fields of the Prairie Provinces make it possible to use large, modern combine harvesters.

Huge salmon like these in British Columbia are a valuable catch.

The hot sunny summers in Quebec help tomatoes ripen for harvesting.

On Land and Sea

Fishing is a very large and important industry in Canada. From the earliest days of Canada's history, fishing has provided food and trade for Canadians.

Canada's first fisheries were off its eastern shores in the Atlantic Ocean. These waters are still important fishing grounds and are filled with cod, lobsters, and crabs. Newfoundland and Nova Scotia are the centers of the fishing industry in eastern Canada.

Canada's Pacific waters are also important fishing grounds. Salmon is the most valuable fish harvested in these waters. British Columbia is the western center of Canada's fishing industry.

In the far north, fishing is still a major source of food for the Inuit. Because the lakes and rivers in this part of Canada are frozen for much of the year, the Inuit have to cut or drill through the ice to start fishing.

Farming is another major industry in Canada. Most Canadian farms are owned and operated by families. In addition to the vast amounts of wheat grown on the Prairies, Canadian farmers also raise many other crops. In Ontario, many different fruits and vegetables are raised. The Okanagan Valley in British Columbia is known for its apples.

City Life

Almost eight out of every ten Canadians live in cities. Toronto is Canada's largest city. More than three million people live there. The city is a major business center. In Toronto, the Canadian National Tower is the world's largest self-supporting structure. It is 1,821 feet high.

Montreal is Canada's second largest city. It is also the second largest French-speaking city in the world after Paris, France. Montreal is actually built on an island where the St. Lawrence and Ottawa rivers meet. The city was once the center of Canada's fur trade. It has many important businesses and industries. The city is famous for its theaters and concerts. Thousands of tourists visit Montreal every year.

Quebec was the capital of Canada when it was ruled by the French. Today, Quebec still has the stone walls built by the French to protect the city. Quebec is a much smaller city than Toronto and Montreal.

Canada has many other cities. Ottawa is the country's national capital. It is a modern city with tall buildings of glass and steel. Vancouver on Canada's west coast is the country's third largest city. It is one of Canada's major port cities.

The fantastic Château Frontenac in Quebec stands high above the St. Lawrence River.

Jacques Cartier Square is in the old part of Montreal, which was founded by the French in 1642.

Canada is governed from a majestic Parliament building in Ottawa.

Sports

Canadians love all kinds of sports. The great open countryside is good for hiking, skiing, mountain climbing, ice hockey, and fishing. In summer, baseball, tennis, and golf are popular with many Canadians. Lacrosse is a national sport. It comes from a Native American game and is played throughout Canada.

Water sports such as white-water rafting, canoeing, waterskiing, and sailing attract many Canadians. On weekends, Canadians often travel to cottages or camping grounds near lakes and rivers to enjoy water sports. Canada also has many national parks where people can hike, climb mountains, and see the natural beauty of the country.

Canadians love ice hockey, which is played by Canadians of all ages on both outdoor and indoor ice. Professional ice hockey is very popular in Canada. Many of the best players in the National Hockey League are Canadians.

Baseball is popular in Canada. There are two major league baseball teams in Canada. They are the Montreal Expos and the Toronto Blue Jays. The Blue Jays won the World Series in 1992. Canadians also play soccer and their own game of football.

When winter comes, rivers and lakes freeze solid. Ice hockey is a favorite winter sport.

In summer many Canadians enjoy water sports such as boating.

Canadian football is played from July to November.

Famous Landmarks

Niagara Falls is one of the most popular vacation spots for both Canadians and other visitors.

In Autumn the maple trees in the Ontario forests turn many shades of red and yellow. It is a beautiful sight that is famous throughout the world.

The famous emerald waters of Lake Louise with ice-covered Mount Victoria in the background.

Beautiful Mount Edith Cavell is named after a World War I nurse. It is 11,033 feet high.

The Calgary Stampede attracts many visitors and is a reminder that cattle ranching is still important today.

The Canadian National (CN) Tower in Toronto is the world's tallest self-supporting tower. It is 1,821 feet high.

Facts and Figures

Canada-the Land and People

Population:	26,620,500
Area:	3,851,809 square miles
Capital City:	Ottawa
Largest City: Population:	Toronto 3,427,000
Official Languages:	French and English
Religion:	Christian; but others are practiced
Money:	Canadian Dollar ($) $1 = .81 (U.S.)
Highest Mountain:	Mount Logan, 19,850 ft.

Provinces and Territories

Territories	Capital Cities
Yukon	Whitehorse
Northwest Territories	Yellowknife
Provinces	
British Columbia	Vancouver
Alberta	Edmonton
Saskatchewan	Regina
Manitoba	Winnipeg
Ontario	Toronto
Quebec	Quebec City
Newfoundland	St. Johns
Nova Scotia	Halifax
Prince Edward Island	Charlottetown

Major Public Holidays

New Year's Day	January 1
Good Friday	Friday before Easter
Victoria Day	Fourth Monday in May
Canada Day	July 1
Labor Day	First Monday in September
Thanksgiving Day	Second Monday in October
Christmas Day	December 25

Special Provincial Holidays

St. John the Baptist (Quebec)	June 24
Discovery Day (Yukon)	Third Monday in August
St. Patrick's Day	Monday nearest March 17

Average Temperatures in Fahrenheit

City (Province/Territory)	January	June
Toronto (Ontario)	24°F	71°F
Dawson City (Yukon)	−13°F	66°F
Churchill (Manitoba)	−4°F	59°F
Edmonton (Alberta)	10°F	75°F
Montreal (Quebec)	14°F	77°F
Halifax (Nova Scotia)	25°F	66°F

Further Reading

Books

Anderson, Joan. *Pioneer Settlers of New France.* Dutton Children's, 1990

Brickenden, Jack. *We Live in Canada.* Watts, 1984

Canadian Childhoods: A Tundra Anthology. Tundra Books, 1989

Haskins, Jim. *Count Your Way Through Canada.* Carolrhoda, 1989

Holling, Holling C. *Paddle-to-the-Sea.* Houghton Mifflin, 1980

Le Vert, Suzanne. *Canada.* Chelsea, 1992

Redekopp, Elsa. *Dream and Wonder: A Child's View of Canadian Village Life.* Kindred Press, 1986

Sabin, Louis. *Canada.* Troll, 1985

Audio-Visuals

Audio Cassettes

Mahoney, Judy. *Teach Me French.* Teach Me Tapes, Inc., Minneapolis, MN, 1985

Index